MW01245797

DIALOGUE
A WAY TO LIVE
REVISED EDITION

Irving R. Stubbs

Palmetto Publishing Group
Charleston, SC

Dialogue: A Way to Live - Revised Edition
Copyright © 2020 by Irving R. Stubbs

The Living Dialog™ Ministries

First Edition

Printed in the United States

ISBN-13: 978-1-64990-088-3

CONTENTS

www.Dialogue4Us.com

PREFACE

Leaders shape culture. Leaders model communication. Leaders empower followers. History validates the irrefutable role of leadership. I have decades of experience with leaders. We used dialogue to solve problems and make things happen. If dialogue is to have an impact on the cultures in which we live, it will be because leaders led this mission.

I became aware of the benefits of dialogue at Davidson College. As a small group of us entered our senior year, we recognized an interest in political science, but had no time to take those courses. We asked a professor if he would meet with us to help us learn what we could about political science. He agreed. He found other professors interested in joining us.

There were no final authorities, no grades, and no dumb questions. Professors and students explored together. We found insights, including answers to questions we might not have asked in the classroom. We listened to one another with open minds. We gained knowledge about political science that stretched our thinking.

This book is about a way to live. It is not a "new and improved" way. It has been around for a long time. However, my assumption, based on many years of observation, is that only a small percentage of leaders and the population practice this way. **What would it be like if leaders led 12% of us to practice dialogue described in this book?**

The practice is challenging. It will take leadership to stretch the practice to levels that will have optimum impact. The Dialogue Leadership Institute described in the Appendix can be a fulcrum to leverage that potential.

Irving Stubbs

CHAPTER 1:
INTRODUCTION

A TRUE STORY

Jack led the growth of a now multi-billion-dollar company. The Board of Directors employed him to be an outside
CEO and Chairman of a family business. He changed the
name, expanded the product line and built a new corporate headquarters. He increased employees by 125%,
sales by 222% and the value of the stock increased by
300%. We were friends and colleagues in another corporation. Jack invited me to become his consultant.

We evolved the practice of dialogue throughout the company. Jack and I had dialogue prior to executive retreats
that I was to facilitate. We assigned a serous book to be
read that included the importance of dialogue. We engaged in why and how to practice dialogue. We focused
on issues in a dialogue context including matters such as
the most effective integration of a new acquisition.

Jack viewed the practice of values to be an essential part of the culture of the company. This practice became a signature feature of the company.

There were examples of breaches in the practice of those core values and those involved were fired. There were times when dialogue was not appropriate.

I asked Jack what he thought the benefits were of the practice of dialogue in his company. Here is what he said: "Getting the pertinent facts and potential alternatives was one of the best benefits of dialogue. Team members recognized that their ideas were considered and their input was important. We could see that each member had some segment of the best solution and collectively the final decision was the best possible.

"The dialogue discipline enhanced communications on strategic issues and growth opportunities. It engaged the leadership team in positive and creative work sessions where everyone contributed in an open fashion and multiple aspects of a situation could be examined."

WHAT IS DIALOGUE?

We would NOT be in dialogue in interpersonal or group relationships if I focused on showing you how wrong you are or tried to persuade you to accept my point of view without being willing to listen to your point of view.

We are in a dialogue environment when we listen for what is meant and respond empathetically, when we ask questions to clarify and draw out the thinking of others, when we resist being defensive, when we agree to disagree when called for but seek to find that on which we do agree, when we don't focus to persuade but to discover, when we change our views or positions in light of what we are discovering.

Transformational Dialogue is a means to constructive convergence and synergistic relationships.

Converge:
to come together and unite in a common interest or focus
(Merriam-Webster)
to tend to meet in a point or line; incline toward each other
(Dictionary.com)

Synergy:
a mutually advantageous conjunction or compatibility of distinct business participants or elements (such as resources or efforts)
(Merriam-Webster)
the interaction of elements that when combined produce a total effect that is greater than the sum of the individual elements
(Dictionary.com)

CHAPTER 2:
EXAMPLES

ROGER

Roger was Jewish, German, and a leading engineer in England. His family migrated to England after Hitler's rule in Germany. He asked me to help him with a challenge.

He was to consolidate three companies that were competitors in a global business. Their headquarters were in France, Wales, and the U.S. Employees, plants, products, patents, offices, customers, and cultures were to be integrated for a competitive advantage in their worldwide business.

The company leaders could be *ordered* to make the consolidation happen. Roger needed the leaders to contribute to sustainable contributions and motivation. A different approach was needed.

I had consulted with Roger's parent company. During that time, we had a weekend break. Roger asked me if there was something in Europe that I would like to do on that weekend. I asked him if we could visit the cathedral in Chartres, France.

In college, medieval history was a special interest. Henry Adams' classic *Mont-Saint-Michel and Chartres* fascinated me. The thought of visiting Chartres was intriguing and Roger said, "Let's do that."

It was a great weekend. There was the incongruity of a German Jew and an American Protestant making a "pilgrimage" to a Roman Catholic cathedral. It was that incongruity that stimulated serious dialogue between us and prepared the way for our project.

The project was a challenge. Nevertheless, with shuttle diplomacy and substantive dialogue with each group, we built the bridges to make the consolidation happen. We celebrated success in a meeting with the key people from each group. There was satisfaction, ownership, and commitment to future progress that made the effort worthwhile.

THE JURY IS IN

A company, with a long history of making a particular product, recognized the need for a new product line. Unknowns clouded the decisions. A colleague and I recommended a process we had learned about from a mentor friend. A multi-day off-site meeting included several company disciplines and even corporate directors.

The model was based on a jury trial. Pro and con advo-cates and experts came with data to make their cases. Directors and senior executives comprised the jury. The purpose was not to make a decision but to surface fea-tures to be considered. The decision makers followed with dialogue to reshape the company's direction.

JL

A client's CEO directed me to "orient" JL, a new senior executive, to the culture of his new business home. At his first executive meeting at that new home, JL and I took a walk during which I did the orientation, and we discov-ered that we could be open and trusting with each other. We bonded.

Later, JL became the CEO of another corporation. He in-vited me to be his consultant. We evolved a unique plan. We visited major company locations to convey the plan to key managers. At dinner meetings, JL shared the plan and then responded to questions.

Something came up in the first meeting, and JL respond-ed in a way I thought was not in sync with the intention of our visit. After the meeting, JL and I met. I shared my concern. He was the person in charge. His executive power would prevail. However, he was willing to listen to my concern. We engaged in serious dialogue.

At breakfast with the group the next morning, I was sur-prised to hear JL say that he wished to reposition what he had said the night before. Our dialogue made a difference. His people sensed that their CEO was open to revised thinking, and our plans for the subsequent meetings were on a sounder footing.

THE RELOCATION ISSUE

I was asked to facilitate a workshop with the leaders of a Canadian company to deal with the relocation of a manufacturing plant. There was conflict among the key people about how and where to relocate.

We used an analytical tool to sort out the forces that impacted this decision. I asked many questions to clarify the analysis. Listening to responses and cooling some of them in order to clarify the meaning of the exchanges proved to be of value.

The workshop went on for most of a day. The questions to be answered at this meeting were posted up front to remind us why we were there. Namely *when, where, and how* shall we relocate this plant?

By the end of the day, there were serious conversations about these concerns. Clarity came when the key executive took the floor and said something to this effect: "What has become clear today is that we should not relocate this plant. We will focus on acting on what has emerged from this workshop to strengthen our plant where it is."

Business leaders, in my experience, see the benefits of dialogue.

Is dialogue always appropriate? No

Does it always work? No

Are there barriers? Yes

But the benefits outweigh the barriers.

CHAPTER 3:
BENEFITS

Many benefits of practicing transformational dialogue surfaced in previous and will surface in following chapters. In this chapter, we highlight six pivotal benefits.

DIALOGUE IS A MEANS TO TAP INTO TACIT KNOWLEDGE.

Hungarian scientist Michael Polanyi viewed knowledge understood or implied without stating it, to be an important form of knowing.

Polanyi wrote in *The Tacit Dimension* that we should start from the fact that *"we can know more than we can tell."* He called this phase of knowing *tacit knowledge.* He affirmed that in tacit knowledge there was hidden truth worth exploring.

Polanyi identified dialogue as a way to discover the hidden truths of tacit knowledge. In a heuristic field, the nearness of discovery prompts the mind toward it. This approach to knowledge is the mainspring of originality and, by implication, innovation.

DIALOGUE CONNECTS US AS PERSONS.

How do we know each other? Is it what we look like? The clothes we wear? The schools we attended? The jobs we've had? The clubs we belong to?

If we wish to relate to others at a deeper level, dialogue achieves this benefit. Physician-psychologist Paul Tournier wrote a seminal book entitled *The Meaning of Persons*. In it he made the following declaration: "I can speak endlessly of myself, to myself or to someone else, without ever succeeding in giving a complete and truthful picture of myself."

There remains in each of us, he adds, "something of impenetrable mystery." We cannot grasp the true reality of ourselves or of others, "but only an image; a fragmentary and deformed image, an appearance: the 'personage.'" He differentiates the personage, which we present as "actors in a play," from the persons that we truly are. Tournier: "The person is the original creation."

Tournier believed that dialogue liberates us as persons. "In this act of dialogue in which a relationship involves both choice and risk and lays us open to an exchange of replies, we act with a responsibility that further opens us as persons."

DIALOGUE OPENS CLOSED SYSTEMS.

After 9/11 we learned that if our multiple intelligence sources had been more open with one another, available information might have warned us about what the jihadists were planning.

Instead of walls between groups, like marketing, production, and finance, *open systems management* views separations between groups as being semi-permeable membranes through which information, personnel, and energy can be exchanged easily.

A team of research scientists located in Switzerland experienced limits in gaining patents for their work. Gaining patents involved patent attorneys. Research-driven patents were key indicators for the success of this group.

I was invited to consult with this group on its patent generation. The group included bright people from half a dozen different countries. I interviewed the group members and spent time with them to understand the work as well as the facility culture. I discovered that the scientists felt most creative in relationships with family and friends rather than in those in their research lab.

At an off-site workshop, we did a number of things; however, it was a game we played that was the key lever for progress. In groups with scientists and attorneys in each group, one person was designated to role-play being a patent. Group members asked the "patent" many different kinds of questions. It was a fun experience that thawed barriers and energized creativity.

Groups working on specific patent issues followed the exercise. Exchanges across domains were needed to refine the patent process. Dialogue opened up those exchanges. The simple game led to a culture change, which led to solutions in the interests of all.

DIALOGUE STIMULATES A LARGER INTELLIGENCEWITH WHICH TO DEAL WITH HEAVY SOCIETAL ISSUES.

When she was a graduate student and a member of the research staff at the Conflict Research Consortium at the University of Colorado, Boulder, Michelle Maiese wrote about challenges dealing with public conflicts. She said that those involved in public conflicts often "tend to cling to their own positions and denigrate views of the opposing side, rarely ask each other questions or genuinely listen to what the other side is saying, tend to stereotype each other and misunderstand each other's positions, causing each participant to become increasingly polarized, block effective communication because of competition, prejudice, and fear."

"Dialogue," said Maiese, "surfaces assumptions so deeply embedded in our worldviews that we might not recognize them. These assumptions include those rooted in culture, race, religion, and economic background. ...

Participants in dialogue wish to see what can be discovered in their encounters with others.

"Rather than reacting in a hostile way to each other's opinions, parties must examine the meaning of these opposing opinions and assumptions. ... Suspending assumptions makes people aware of their thought processes and brings about an enhanced level of consciousness."

At the end of his book *On Dialogue,* David Bohm shares why we may find it difficult to exploit the potential of this benefit of dialogue.

He reminds us that half a million years ago people lived in small groups of hunter-gatherers; they all knew one another and used what Bohm called "literal" thought only for simple technical purposes. "But then came the agricultural revolution, and larger societies developed. These societies needed much more organization and order and technology, and they had to use much more literal thought.

"They organized society by saying, 'You belong here, you do this, you do that.' They began, therefore, to treat everything as a separate object, including other people. They used people as means to an end."

"Such thought then entered into the relationship between countries. Each country treated the other country as an object, which was to be controlled, or fought over, or defeated."

"Literal thought knows the person by his function – he is whatever you call him – a worker, a banker, this or that. That sets up the social hierarchy – people are isolated from each other, and the participation is very limited."

"In such a view, the world is made of objects, literally. We treat other people as objects, and eventually you must treat yourself as an object, saying, 'I must fit in here, and I must do this and be that and become better,' or whatever. But 'society' is not an objective reality – period. It is a reality created by all the people through their consciousness."

It is in a dialogue environment, Bohm believed, that people are understood to be different, and this must be respected if heavy societal issues are to be dealt with.

DIALOGUE STRETCHES OUR LEVELS OF CONSCIOUSNESS.

What we watch, listen to, think, and remember bind together to create consciousness. Our consciousness is like a symphony orchestra with multiple players combining their talents to create a performance.

Our consciousness plays a big role in our capacity for and practice of dialogue. These three-pound brains in our heads contain billions of neurons with trillions of synaptic connections. These electro-chemical connections flash across our brain networks and form patterns that lead to our consciousness.

Our levels of consciousness evolve. They stretch from early childhood, youth and adulthood to meet our needs at those stages in our lives. As we become adults, we become more aware of others around us. If and when we evolve to the higher levels of consciousness, a more inclusive and relational life flourishes. We are less self-centered. We are more open. The orchestra members create music between the notes. We are more receptive to practice dialogue.

Developmental psychologists suggest that only a small percentage of the population reach this higher level. They believe that there are steps we can take to raise our levels of consciousness. The practice of transformational dialogue enables those steps.

DIALOGUE GETS US CLOSER TO REALITY.

With higher levels of consciousness, we become more inclusive and open to development. Getting to know one another as persons beyond the "garments" we wear – discovering tacit knowledge, the stuff below the surface – opening up closed systems in which different functions and expertise stimulate collaboration and innovation – and finding a larger intelligence with which to deal with heavy societal issues are ways to get us closer to reality.

After many years of marriage, five children, and a lot of dialogue, I discovered a depth of love that gave our marriage relationship an enduring joy; I have had clients for whom our desired outcomes were not always what we hoped for, but based on our dialogical approach to reality, we continued our relationship because we knew that more success would come if we persevered; and, like Job in the Bible, there were times when my spiritual faith through my dialogue with God emerged with the discovery that I had been grasped by an ultimate reality that has sustained and empowered me. Dialogue is a means to get us closer to that reality.

However, not all of us want to face our reality.

> *Go, go, go, said the bird: human kind*
> *Cannot bear very much reality.*
> *Time past and time future*
> *What might have been and what has been*
> *Point to one end, which is always present.*
> T. S. Eliot – *Burnt Norton*

In research published in the *Journal of Economic Psychology,* biologist Robert Trivers finds that we unrealistically deceive ourselves in order to deceive others to gain a social advantage. We employ biased information gathering, biased reasoning and biased recollections to support what we want to believe and avoid that which does not support our beliefs.

What kinds of leaders promote reality in science, religion, politics, marketing, or annual reports? If dialogue is a means to get us closer to reality, maybe we have a clue for why it seems that only a small percentage of the population advocates and practices the kind of dialogue described in this book.

Medical doctor, neurologist, and neuroscientist, David O. Wiebers wrote *Theory of Reality: Evidence for Existence Beyond the Brain and Tools for Your Journey.* What he affirms about reality at a cosmic level is a stretch for most of us. His theory includes references to consciousness, quantum theory, an implicit order, and other matters to which citations in this book have alluded.

If a benefit of dialogue that transforms us is that it gets us closer to reality, then these gleanings from Wiebers invite a level of dialogue that could change our worldviews.

Decades of research seem to confirm that we live in a universe of energy. Our senses put us in touch with an explicit material order. The implicit order of complex energy is stretching our understanding of reality as we make discoveries through intuition, peak experiences, meditation and near-death-experiences.

Wiebers, the neuroscientist, explores the reality of consciousness as yet another dimension of reality with big implications. "Intelligent, informative consciousness is fundamental to all matter," says Wiebers, and "The universe is a unified living process rather than a collection of separate objects." Furthermore, adds Wiebers, "Consciousness is the canvas upon which mind generates our impressions – it is not PART of the impressions." "The deepest reality is the reality of pure consciousness."

"Despite the human brain having an enormous number of neurons (nerve cells) and synapses (connections between brain nerve cells), there is substantial evidence from the realms of computer science and neuroscience over the past couple of decades presented by Berkovich (1993), Romijn (1997) and others to suggest that the brain's anatomical and functional total storage capacity is incompatible with the possibility of storing a lifetime of memories.

"This would suggest that our memories, which are part of the contents of our consciousness ... would need to exist outside the realm of physical brain structures."

Getting one's consciousness, "free from the endless stream of 'waking chatter' and the 'noise' of day-to-day living ... enhances one's coherence." "When one intentionally chooses to bring higher-level motivations into the experience (e.g., love, compassion, selflessness, forgiveness, acceptance, gratitude), as opposed to lower-level motivations (fear, guilt, greed, revenge, selfishness, jealousy), one becomes more coherent and open to other layers of higher-level consciousness/information/ intelligence that would otherwise be inaccessible."

"Everyone has the potential to make use of it, and the results can constitute some of the most wondrous and beautiful experiences in an individual's lifetime, as well as some of the most profound and helpful revelations that any of us can contribute." Wiebers, the medical doctor, affirms that this heightened experience of consciousness contributes to good health and well-being.

Wiebers' theology would not likely be popular in most religious institutions, but he views this reality of the stretch-consciousness to relate to a divine energy.

And, the value-add to this journey with David Wiebers includes these words: "I think, then, that there is the possibility of the transformation of consciousness, both individually and collectively. It's important that it happens together - it's got to be both. And, therefore, this whole question - of communication and the ability to **dialogue,** the ability to participate in communication - is crucial."

CHAPTER 4:
ANALYSIS

In the opinion survey on the practice of dialogue that my colleague Farheen Naveed and I conducted, educators, psychologists, religious leaders, social workers, business leaders and others from five nations responded.

The responses revealed that cultures influence receptivity for dialogue. In some cultures, there is little knowledge of dialogue and therefore little receptivity. Some cultures discourage dialogue. There are cultures in which there are no barriers to the practice of dialogue.

The survey included the definition of dialogue, presented previously:

We are in a dialogue environment when we listen for what is meant and respond empathetically to what we hear, when we ask questions to clarify and draw out the thinking of others, when we resist being defensive, when we acknowledge that on which we disagree, but seek to find that on which we do agree, when we try to discover more than to persuade, when we find ourselves changing our views or positions in light of what we are discovering.

The survey employed Kurt Lewin's change model. In this model, countervailing forces squeeze to a "quasi-stationary equilibrium" (QSE) a status quo thought of as a conceptual spring that gets tighter as the forces impinge. Change toward the goal requires an increase in "driving forces" to overpower the "restraining forces" and/or a thawing of the "restraining forces" to allow the "driving forces" to make progress toward the goal.

The lists that follow are composites of multiple sources including responses to the survey. The list includes redundancies retained for their nuances.

DRIVING FORCES

Socrates was happy to be refuted by inquiry because in that challenge to his previous views, he was relieved of the burden of false opinion.

"In dialogue, we penetrate behind the polite superficialities and defenses in which we habitually armor ourselves. We listen and respond to one another with an authenticity that forges a bond between us." (Daniel Yankelovich)

"Being open to meeting someone different from yourself and taking part in a collision of ideas is what is dear to me in being human." (Carole Harris)

"For a democracy to remain robust, we need constantly to bump into people with colliding perspectives and points of view." (Cass Sunstein)

"When we suspend assumptions and think together, our sensitivity becomes a fine net able to gather subtle meanings." (Peter Senge)

Practicing transformational dialogue connects us as persons more than personages, demonstrates love, is a means by which God's Spirit opens us to liberating Truth, opens closed systems, is a means to tacit knowledge, stretches our levels of consciousness, stimulates a larger intelligence with which to deal with heavy societal issues, bridges gaps, bonds for harmony, and builds things.

When dialogue is sustained long enough for internalization, it becomes an adventure, a source of energy and joy. It increases empathy, helps build interpersonal relationships and reduces stress, helps to better understand one another that can reduce the barriers we erect between ourselves and those we see as other.

We reach new insights, experience co-creativity, and solve problems with greater depth. It provides peace within, with others, and with God. It enhances our emotional intelligence, helps in therapy groups.

In one sense it is the best way to come unto and become a new being in Christ Jesus. Those that practice it, enjoy a more complete (Holy) life. The experience of satisfaction at the opening of one's mind to a new reality is rewarding. It strengthens courage to speak and share, enhances insight, helps to build character - enables the development of trust and honesty, helps to cure the disease of loneliness that has been identified as a major problem in today's society.

Human minds are the most powerful device in this world and the most complicated. Dialogue is the unwiring mechanism of this complex device. It enables people to feel they are in a "safe" and non-judgmental space that allows diverse opinions, and freedom to express opinions that might run counter to the majority, supports the principle of freedom of speech, produces synergy, upholds the principal that clarity is more important than agreement, helps to see the bigger picture.

It is like a catalyst that helps us grow as a society, enables servant leadership, is a way of exploring the roots of the many crises faced by society today, builds communities of mutual trust and interests.

Rather than "I" it brings us to "We."

It energizes worldviews based on *shalom* including peace, harmony, wholeness, justice, and joy, provides a foundation for long-term norms to exchange different ideas and settle conflicts, transforms ideas to realities and empowers by shaping and converting stone-age to tech-age. **As dialogue slows down normal communication, there is an inclination to dig deeper.**

Just imagine what could be accomplished if political foes could discuss options and compromise without all the grandstanding and rhetoric, which simply fuels the general population's behaviors. It could stem the tide of individual acts of violence caused by frustration, iso-lation, and mental illness gone unnoticed/untreated. It also **encourages participants to be less likely to accept extremist leaders.**

Practicing transformational dialogue is viewed by many as a very positive force. However, there are forces that restrain that practice.

RESTRAINING FORCES

What follows is a list of conditions and points of view that may either prevent or restrain the practice of trans-formational dialogue.

- The meaning and benefits of dialogue are not clearly understood.

- Participants lack empathy with and respect for others.

- People avoid engaging in dialogue based on feel-ings of weakness.

- Active learning skills are lacking.

- There is confirmation bias; we only hear what others who agree with us say.

- When there is fear of being rejected or criticized, it is safer to keep quiet and not engage in dialogue.

- The inability to suspend judgment and honor cultural differences is widespread.

- Insistence on being in charge and setting unrealistic goals prior to dialogue is encouraged by authority figures.

- In some areas of the world, leaders are discouraged from promoting or initiating dialogue, and women are not allowed to speak openly.

- Dialogue has the potential to change its participants, and many people are afraid of change.

- Many religious as well as political leaders create closed environments that negate others' thoughts and opinions.

SELECTED SURVEY COMMENTS

Below is a list of comments selected from our opinion survey on the practice of dialogue.

Dialogue has the potential to solve many national and international problems.

To be effective worldwide, dialogue skills must be taught throughout educational systems in all countries and to all age groups.

Dialogue leads to peace, and the absence of dialogue leads to war.

Avoiding dialogue may be seen as a way to avoid conflict.

Creating safe, secure environments without fear and without barriers will promote the practice of dialogue.

Social gatherings that might promote dialogue instead result in everyone busily responding to what's on their phone devices.

We talk **about** each other more than we talk **to** each other. We talk and talk and talk, but we do not know how to engage in authentic conversation.

Those in authority stifle dialogue when they encourage polarization by expressing and insisting upon only one point of view.

Our society promotes a reliance on "experts" rather than opening up to different ideas and perspectives from everyone.

Social media encourages reacting rather than thinking, evaluating, and understanding.

Dialogue is a healthy activity that enhances and develops one's intellect through listening to others' opinions and being challenged to see reality in a different way.

The preceding thoughts from multiple sources and cultures affirm that **the world needs dialogue**.

THIS ANALYSIS IMPLIES ASSUMPTIONS.

The practice of transformational dialogue includes anthropology, psychology, theology, philosophy, sociology, and economics.

There is a shortage of the serious practice of transformational dialogue in the world today.

We need a means to sustain this practice.

This is a leadership issue.

To reduce the restraining forces:

1. Leadership is needed to use its commitment and influence to stretch the practice of dialogue.

2. Public relations' initiatives are needed to convey the nature and benefits of practicing dialogue and to make a broader public aware of how and where to gain the skills for practicing dialogue.

3. Dialogue training tools are needed.

4. An umbrella is needed for dialogue organizations to connect and synergize.

5. A means is needed to encourage and support educational systems to include dialogue in their curriculum.

6. A means is needed to offer support for the practice of dialogue in receptive international cultures.

7. A means must be found to sustain support for the practice of dialogue.

THE APPENDIX OFFERS A MEANS TO ADDRESS THESE NEEDS.

Note: The content of this chapter from multiple sources was very complex. I am indebted to Jacqueline Stevens who took the raw material, translated it, edited it, and brought it to the level of coherence that we are able to read above.

CHAPTER 5:
FRIENDS

I asked these friends to tell me what our dialogue meant to them.

Carole is a university professor. I learned new things when I read some of her publications. This discovery prompted exchanges in which both of us began to see some things from new perspectives.

Carole used articles written by her students for a school publication to engage these students in dialogue. I remembered Jane Vella, who pointed to what she called "quantum education." (Vella 1994)

I asked Carole if she felt we had experienced dialogue in our relationship. Here is her response. "Irving and I met in August 2017 after two different family friends from my father's home town suggested, independently one from the other, that I reach out to him. So, I did.

"In our first conversations, I learned all about how Irving had worked closely with my father's childhood friend, whom I also knew and loved growing up. How satisfying it was to picture this family friend anew from Irving's perspective!

"Hearing Irving's stories, which were often quite funny, was like a window opening up on someone who felt like part of my family, and someone who was deeply connected to my father. Irving's stories expanded my perspective on my father, his boyhood friend, and the generation in which they grew up.

"Irving has shared stories about any number of consultation jobs he was asked to take on where the parties involved were attempting to achieve a goal or rectify a problem, and from what he reported, you could never imagine a solution, so heated were the disagreements.

"These stories stretched my capacity to live with the discomfort of disagreement and see it as part of a process. I admire and appreciate Irving's attitude of hanging in there in the midst of conflict, as well as his understanding that heated arguments may very well be an opening outward to a genuine exchange of ideas.

"Through listening to one another, the parties involved might break through to something bigger than themselves. Irving's commitment to digging deeper and seeing things through to meaningful communication seems to have a spiritual quality to me, one that is sorely needed in our times.

"Irving and I may be opposites in terms of politics (I don't know!), but I agree with him that our world has become dangerously polarized, with people gravitating mostly to others that are like minded. I believe the Internet exacerbates this problem and is at heart, potentially, quite un-democratic.

"I agree with political philosopher Cass Sunstein who feels that for a democracy to remain robust, we need constantly to bump into people with colliding perspectives and points of view. (Sunstein 2017)

"Being open to meeting someone different from yourself and taking part in a collision of ideas is what is dear to me in being human, and I've found a kindred soul in Irving. I feel blessed."

Harry is an attorney and a friend of many years. We read heavy science and theology together. We dig into our readings with joy and enlightenment. His contribution tells our story.

"The question is whether true dialogue is worth the effort? The answer is yes, because true dialogue is transformational.

"Most conversations are shallow and do not reach the depth necessary to be qualified as dialogue. For those who have truly participated in and understand dialogue, good questions lead to deeper questions.

"The reason is additional questions require those who are communicating to be sure first that the meaning of the question is understood in order for the meaning of the answer to be understood. The thought processes for the additional questions to the initial question is the reason that dialogue is transformational.

"The series of questions makes dialogue participants consider a greater foundational meaning for the entire subject. This transforms the original question into something greater than what one initially intended.

"One of the reasons that I know this is true is because of my experience in dialogue with Irving Stubbs for over 40 years. During this time, we have regularly discussed important subjects and most times have utilized dialogue to discuss the subjects deeply.

"As these events continued, so did our skills at asking questions and participating in dialogue. This resulted in a process of delving deeper into the nature of the meaning of true and complete communication. The result opened our minds to more possibilities of a greater understanding of the meaning of the subject matter and the potential answers.

"The result for my part has been mind-expanding and an understanding of the richer fabrics of meaning and truth. The 'aha' moment occurs at the point when the consideration of another question opens one's mind to a different picture or perspective of the subject matter.

"For my part it feels like another layer of my brain has been opened to a greater consciousness. One can sense that on such occasions, one grows into and becomes a newer and more whole (holier) Being."

(Perhaps from his legal training and experience, Harry makes an important connection between dialogue and questions. Open-ended questions clearly open to greater consciousness and "aha" moments when a flow of questions lead to rich and enriching insights.)

Jacqueline has been a friend and colleague for decades. She was a professor of criminal justice. Her IQ is likely higher than mine. I asked her to share what she thought was the basis of our dialogue. "That one is easy, Irving: **Love** - a deep appreciation of the other and a recognition of a common bond to make things better in the world.

"It began for me when I interviewed for the job at your company. You gave me a personality test that consisted of questions - the answers to which would tell you something deeper about me. I felt at home with your endeavor, and I remember thinking, 'Irving Stubbs really understands what is important not only in a relationship (dialogue), but also in a person.' You made me feel comfortable and welcome. You weren't looking for someone who agreed with you, but someone who shared your values of integrity - a seeker of truth and, I believe, of justice.

"I also felt at home with you because you appeared to care deeply about what you were doing. Putting all of that together equaled the potential for a deep friendship, a common road traveled and grounded in CARE.

"My studies at Vanderbilt were focused on Martin Heidegger's *Being and Time.* Heidegger's philosophy of being-in-the-world as *Dasein* (being there, as in being at the horizon or end of life - living with a grounded and deep sense of one's mortality) was a shared reality between us, as it has been for other friendships in my life. For Heidegger, we live in advance of ourselves. We carry our end within us. How we live that truth of being mortal is literally the difference between living authentically or inauthentically. (Heidegger 1962)

"You and I share a reality that is not designed or concocted by us, but that simply is. It is not easy to put into words, yet it is manifested through dialogue."

I asked television personality, author of *You Bet Your Life,* and friend of many years, **Spencer Christian**, how he would describe the dialogue in our relationship. With his permission, here is his response.

"I found our dialogue meaningful, not only because of the words and ideas exchanged during the dialogue, but also because of the probing 'internal dialogue' that has naturally followed our conversations.

"My dialogue with you has always encouraged me to more carefully examine my relationship with God, to question whether I am living purposefully."

In a pastorate, *koinonia* groups of members were formed. (*Koinonia* means fellowship and communion.) A lay couple facilitated each group. The group meetings included dialogue about issues of the members' mutual concerns.

My wife and I met with the facilitators of these groups to listen to their experiences and to help them where we could. The facilitators brought heavy issues to our meetings. They looked to me for answers and support. It turned out that neither my academic degrees, nor my experience were enough. My facilitators were expected to be authentic, and I was obligated to be the same.

As our experience together at the meetings evolved, our relationships changed. We were more honest with one another. We cared more deeply for one another. We got to know ourselves better. And all of this relational honesty, depth, and knowledge paved the way for us to explore heavy questions – questions that did not have simple answers.

In fact, sometimes there were no answers, but just more clarity about the questions. A serious exchange of meaning among us developed as we bonded to help our parishioners.

What did I learn about dialogue from that experience?

We experienced a humility based on a lack of satisfying answers to heavy issues. We experienced a level of empathy that called for trust, caring, and faith. We found resources we did not know were available. We found a sense of belonging that weathered tough times. We discovered transformational dialogue.

This experience happened to me decades ago, but I remember it now with more clarity and gratitude than I remember many other milestones in my life. Transformational dialogue matures you, and it leaves it's mark on you for life.

A 48-minute version of "Bach Out of the Box" (originally "Jack Out of the Box") has more than 1,000 views on YouTube. The concept and performance were the creation of Joseph Erwin, beloved music teacher and choir director. I was the Executive Producer.

Joe was a very close friend for decades. With our wives, we engaged in heavy dialogue on many occasions.

Joe had a dream of presenting Bach in a way to make his music accessible to a wide audience. He asked me to help him realize his dream. The dream's form emerged as a project that would require a church and organist, an orchestra, a chorus, a panel to dialogue about what they heard, a production crew, an editing process, and funding. It took a year to complete the project.

Joe had very strong views about how the production should be. I respected him for his music and concept, but I had strong views about what the product needed to be to gain viewers.

Our dialogue was often a few degrees beyond warm even to a point that I thought I could not continue to produce the project.

Our friendship, mutual respect, shared vision, and creative ways to exchange meaning that required change on both of our parts got us through to the finish line with a product that made us proud and that many have enjoyed. We created music between the notes.

CHAPTER 6:
ADVOCATES

SOCRATES

The philosopher Plato wrote about conversations between Socrates and others. Socrates used dialogue to encourage people to think. He challenged assumptions and forced people to dig deeper for the truths they held. He helped people to surface understandings that they didn't know were there.

Socrates helped fellow citizens discover their "ignorance" and to be morally better. Admonition, persuasion, and advice failed to achieve these goals. He suggested that the job of the dialogue midwife is to develop potential knowledge located in the soul: The "child" being delivered is an undeveloped thought, which has not yet become knowledge. In his dialogue with Socrates, Plato's *Theaetetus* says, "You've made me say far more than ever was in me."

Socrates affirmed that learning is the development of thoughts into "fertile truth." Dialogue refines knowledge, and it is through dialogue that truth emerges. Equated with truth is "the good," and in Socrates' view, inquiry is essential to discover the good.

Therefore, Socrates was happy to be refuted by inquiry because in that challenge to his previous views, he was relieved of the burden of false opinion.

Note: Socrates' search for truth resulted in his arrest and imprisonment. While in prison, he drank a fatal dose of hemlock. Dialogue requires some risk-taking.

DAVID BOHM

Quantum physicist David Bohm, a colleague of Albert Einstein, influenced advocates of dialogue. Science, affirmed Bohm, deals with the explicit order, but there is an ontological reality, which he called the implicit order, that must include three dimensions: the individual, the social, and the cosmic or religious. (Peat 1997)

David Peat wrote Bohm's biography, *Infinite Potential: The Life and Times of David Bohm*. He reported Bohm's affirmation that dialogue occurs when we become open to the flow of a larger intelligence in which we are able to discover the wholeness and interrelatedness of the world. He invited fellow big-thinkers to gather in a "free space" for something new to happen. (Peat 1997)

JOSEPH JAWORSKI

Joseph Jaworski in *Synchronicity - The Inner Path of Leadership,* found in Bohm a kindred spirit. He reported Bohm's view: "We are all connected and operate within living fields of thought and perception. The question to be resolved: How to remove the blocks and tap into that knowledge in order to create the kind of future we all want?" (Jaworski 1996)

DANIEL YANKELOVICH

Pollster and social analyst Daniel Yankelovich in *The Magic of Dialogue: Transforming Conflict into Cooperation* affirmed, "I believe that a certain kind of dialogue holds the key to creating greater cohesiveness among groups of Americans increasingly separated by differences in values, interests, status, politics, professional backgrounds, ethnicity, language, and convictions." He said that a greater mastery of dialogue would advance our civility and our civilization a giant step forward. (Yankelovich 1999)

MARTIN BUBER

Yankelovich reflected on the insights of Jewish philosopher Martin Buber. Buber felt that in dialogue something deeper than conversation goes on.

For Buber, dialogue is a way of being. "In Buber's philosophy, life itself is a form of meeting and dialogue is the 'ridge' on which we meet. In dialogue, we penetrate behind the polite superficialities and defenses in which we habitually armor ourselves. We listen and respond to one another with an authenticity that forges a bond between us." (Yankelovich 1999)

PETER SENGE

Professor Peter Senge introduced the business world to dialogue in *The Fifth Discipline: The Art and Practice of the Learning Organization*. He said that we learn when we suspend assumptions and think together. Our sensitivity becomes a fine net able to gather subtle meanings.

The discipline of team learning, said Senge, starts with *dialogue.* He affirmed that in dialogue there is a cool energy like that associated with a superconductor. With wasted energy (heat) diminished, paradoxically hot topics can be discussed and can become windows to deeper insights. (Senge 1990)

JANE VELLA

Some educators worry that the often well-worn and biased lectures delivered in colleges do not equip the next generations for the practices needed to participate in changing the world. Too much education, argues one educator, involves pedagogic "banking" in which professors make deposits in their students without helping them to learn how to use their knowledge.

Jane Vella designed and led community education and staff development programs in more than 40 countries. She has been a professor and an author. In one of her books, *Learning to Listen, Learning to Teach – The Power of Dialogue in Educating Adults*, she got my attention with her chapter on "Quantum Thinking and Dialogue Education."

Quantum thinking is moving us beyond Newtonian mechanics to a new paradigm. Vella connects dialogue education and quantum thinking. "We have been brought up to accept hierarchy, certainty, cause-and-effect relationships, either-or thinking, and a universe that works as a machine—in short, mechanistic thinking." (Vella 1994)

Vella suggests that it is a shock for most of us to consider a universe composed of energy that is patterned and spontaneous, the certainty of uncertainty, both/and thinking, and the connectedness of everything. "This is quantum thinking." (Vella 1994)

The purpose of dialogue education is to evoke optimal learning. Open questions invite both/and thinking. Many of the principles and practices of dialogue education are designed to raise and sustain the energy of learners.

WILLIAM ISAACS

Professor and author William Isaacs says in his *Dialogue: The Art of Thinking Together:* "Dialogue, as I define it, is a conversation with a center, not sides. It is a way of taking the energy of our differences and channeling it toward something that has never been created before. ... Like the Total Quality Movement, it seeks not to correct defects after they have occurred but to alter processes so that they do not occur in the first place.

"Rather than seeing our conversations as the crashing and careening of billiard balls, individuals may come to see and feel them as fields in which a sense of wholeness can appear, intensify, and diminish in intensity again."

"We cannot manufacture a 'field.' But we can create conditions under which a rich field for interaction is more likely to appear." (Isaacs 1999)

NANCY DIXON

Professor and author Nancy Dixon wrote *Perspectives on Dialogue: Making Talk Developmental for Individuals and Organizations*. She said, "The term 'dialogue' is now frequently heard when the speaker wants to convey that the discussion will be at greater depth or will be more real than usual. Yet, as I listen to conversations between organizational members or sit in meetings of organizations, I hear very little of what I call dialogue going on." (Dixon 1996)

"Dialogue," says Dixon, "requires each person to say one's own truth – not *the* truth but one's own truth." When this happens, each person opens the door to development. "Those who engage in dialogue," affirms Dixon, "must come to it with humility, love, faith, and hope – a formidable list of characteristics, but one that exemplifies a relational, rather than technique, perspective." (Dixon 1996)

Dixon added, "Society to work must be based on shared meaning, which [David] Bohm likened to the cement that holds society together. Dialogue has the potential to alter the meaning each individual holds and, by so doing, is capable of transforming the group, organization, and society." (Dixon 1996)

RICHARD FEYNMAN

Richard Feynman pioneered quantum electrodynamics. He jointly won a Nobel Prize in Physics in 1965. Albert Einstein attended Feynman's first lecture when Feynman was a graduate student at Princeton University, and Bill Gates was so inspired by Feynman's pedagogy that he called him "the greatest teacher I never had." (Gates 2016)

Feynman shared his experience working with a committee of high-powered fellow scientists who were discussing the topic of separating isotopes. He reported on the committee's process.

The process unfolded like this: Someone would make a point; then the chairman would explain a different point of view; then another person would add that there might be another possibility that needed to be considered. Even with considerable disagreement around the table, the chairman did not insist on his point of view.

Feynman was shocked to experience a group of experts building on the ideas of colleagues and sharing many new facets that led to a decision with which there was agreement. There was a confirmation of mutual respect and creative building on a central issue.

KING ABDULLAH II

King Abdullah II of Jordan won the Templeton Prize for promoting dialogue and cooperation between Muslims of different traditions. The Templeton Foundation stated that King Abdullah "has led a reclamation of Islam's moderate theological narrative from the distortions of radicalism." His efforts have "come with great personal cost including condemnation and death threats from radical terrorist groups." (Templeton Foundation 2018)

The King advocated for and funded an initiative named "A Common Word Between Us and You" calling for co-operation between Muslim leaders and their Christian counterparts based on the shared traditions of love of God and neighbor. The King called for the promotion of tolerance, mutual respect, support of inclusion and hope;

to speak out against Islamophobia and other wrongs; and to make our values a real force.

SHIRLEY TURKLE

Sherry Turkle, a professor and author of *Reclaiming Conversation: The Power of Talk in a Digital Age*, offers a perspective about empathy and dialogue.

"When two people are talking, the mere presence of a phone on a table between them or in the periphery of their vision changes both what they talk about and the degree of connection they feel. … People keep the conversation on topics where they won't mind being interrupted. They don't feel as invested in each other." Turkle asks, "What has happened to face-to-face conversation in a world where so many people say they would rather text than talk?" (Turkle 2015)

CONVERSATION DINNERS

In her blog, Christina Ling tells us about *Conversation Dinners*. "Theodore Zeldin is an Oxford scholar who created The Oxford Muse Foundation. … The aim is to rethink the ways in which we communicate with and understand one another. It is not so much a simple conversation as a meeting of minds. … It is to fully engage yourself in a respectful, meaningful conversation, to understand another person in a new way." (Ling 2016)

As a participant in one of these *Dinners*, Ling found that when preconceptions, trifling small talk, and the attempts to impress are stripped down to who we really are, there is openness to transformation. "Authentic conversation *unites* us," concludes Ling. "When we lower our façades and open our minds to the perspectives of others, we allow ourselves to connect and work together on a level we never have before." (Ling 2016)

THE GOD CONNECTION

In a pastorate, I tried to build a unique kind of bridge. In our town there was a manufacturing facility that involved a lot of heavy and noisy machinery. I spent time at that plant tape recording the sounds of the machinery at work. After editing my recording to comprise some rhythmic sounds that had a rough musical quality, I asked my minister of music to compose an organ accompaniment to those sounds. We then presented the composition to the congregation as a *concerto for organ and manufacturing sounds*.

I told the congregants that this strange-sounding "dialogue" was like a bridge between what we often differentiate as being either the sacred or the secular. Our "listening" God, I added, doesn't make that distinction.

This event stirred up conversation in the community, even some dialogue, as well as some questions about this out-of-the-box pastor.

DONALD DAWE

I asked my friend and Christian theologian Donald Dawe what he saw to be the theology of dialogue. He said that dialogue is the means by which God's Spirit opens us to truth.

REUEL HOWE

Reuel Howe was a theologian and author of *The Miracle of Dialogue*. He covered a wide range of reflections that might be considered a theology of dialogue. These were his powerful words: "Dialogue is to love, what blood is to the body." (Howe 1963)

Howe said that dialogue renews vitality to relationships that were originally intended to be life sustaining. He goes *ontological* when he affirms that dialogue brings us into our being. He describes the kind of person whom he calls the "dialogical person." That person is a totally authentic person, an open person, a disciplined person, and a related person. (Howe 1963)

JESUS

In his paper *Jesus and the Samaritan Woman: A Model of Dialogue With The Other,* Nigerian priest Thaddeus Tarhembee offers this insightful interpretation of that relationship. (This paper was an address to his ecclesiastical colleagues convening for a conference.)

"Jesus initiated a dialogue with the 'other,' the Samaritan woman, a non-person in the eyes of the Jews. The 'other' refers to one who differs from another in some respect, like religion or ideology. The 'other' is discriminated against and is not welcomed in that society/group. He/she is despised and rejected by others. This was the situation in which Samaritans found themselves at Jesus' time. The 'other' in our contemporary world is not different from the Samaritan as seen in the gospel."

"Jesus initiated this dialogue to harmonize and heal the wounds of the past, accept those considered outcast/unclean, and to welcome them into the people of God. It is this search for mutual understanding and acceptance that Jesus achieved in the encounter with the Samaritan woman. He is challenging us and inviting us to do the same.

"In a pluralistic society ... we have to meet in conference to search together, listen and learn from each other. This invites us to share with others all that life brings. This sharing should be directed towards what fulfills life and makes people happy. We are all invited to dialogue to enhance mutual understanding, tolerance, trust, acceptance, welcome, and accommodation of 'others.' We are challenged to participate in humankind's corporate self as the creation of God.

"We cannot be truly free unless we are prepared to face the truth. In the posture of dialogue, faith discovers truth... (Herzog). Truth on the other hand will help us to participate honestly and fully in our new corporate relationship." (Tarhembee 2003)

PEGGY NOONAN

Author of *John Paul the Great* and columnist Peggy Noonan shares her dialog experience. "I joined a Christian Bible study group with some intelligent women, who were to one degree or another desperate to believe in something, but it had to be the truth. (They had already tried the non-true, and it hadn't worked.) "These were women who'd been through modern life ... they hadn't kept themselves apart and protected from the culture but had jumped right in, and their conversation was as interesting as a modern novel."

"They all knew that the lives they had previously lived were un-whole, not in accord with the peace that they somehow knew or intuited was out there, and available and summoning." (Noonan 2005)

ART INVITES DIALOGUE

The Virginia Commonwealth University unveiled its Contemporary Art Institute as a non-collecting space for a wide expression of the arts. "The Mending Project" by Taiwanese artist Lee Mingwei was installed in the cathedral-like top-floor gallery of the museum.

About 1,200 spools of thread are arranged up the wall in patterns that create a color field. On the floor is a wooden table with two chairs. At one end of the table is a small pile of neatly folded clothes. On the other end are the chairs. Participant visitors come to this exhibit and take a place at the table opposite a community volunteer who sews and talks with no effort to create a flawless mending object.

You have a conversation with someone you probably never met. Observers have noted animated conversations (dialogues) about all kinds of subjects.

YO-YO MA

Cellist, Yo-Yo Ma, speaks of his music being communion between himself, his instrument, the scores, and his audience. When you watch and listen to him, you become engaged with him as he seeks to be engaged with you. It seems that for Yo-Yo Ma, music is dialogue.

In his *Marsalis on Music* series, Wynton Marsalis and Yo-Yo Ma engaged young students at the Tanglewood Music Center with the challenge of practicing. The last of 12 practicing rules is "connection."

Marsalis and Ma demonstrated connection in an improvisational rendering of Duke Ellington's *Mood Indigo*. I have listened to many renderings of this jazz classic, but this one is a milestone. I could see and hear in this performance the "connections" – the nonverbal exchanges between Marsalis and Ma as they performed with deep empathy and dialogue. They listened to each other, looked at each other, and interpreted each other to bring a fresh meaning of the music to the notes they played.

EMERSON QUARTET

In her Blog *Conversation Matters*, Nancy Dixon, whom we referenced earlier, shared these reflections.

"Last evening, I heard a beautiful reflective conversation between two violins, a viola and a cello. The conversation spoke of the greatest joy and the most profound sorrow, both almost indistinguishable from each other. The conversation was among the members of the world-renowned Emerson Quartet.

"The program was two of Beethoven's late quartets that are enormously difficult to play with sounds ranging from the softest, most delicate in some movements, to rough and strident chords in others. I heard their playing as a conversation because when one instrument introduced a phrase or theme, another voice reflected back a more in-depth statement of that theme, perhaps in a different register or with embellishment, but still recognizable as the same theme.

"It was as though the viola might be saying to the first violin, 'This is the meaning I took from what you just said.' In other passages, the voices of the instruments blended, seeming to have reached a common understanding.

As the music intensified, the players leaned toward each other, just as we lean in when we're concentrating on what a friend is telling us.

"They watched each other, checking to see the right moment to enter the conversation. They even breathed together. At the beginning of a movement, you could see the first violin breathe in before his bow struck the string; the others breathing in concert with him, so that first note from all four instruments was simultaneous.

"The music did not originate from instruments. As beautiful as they are, they were only the carrier. The music came from meaning deep inside each player, in much the same way that the meaning in an authentic conversation arises from deep within each individual speaker." (Dixon 2018)

CHAPTER 7:
METHODOLOGY

To experience dialogue is not like climbing a ladder. It is a nonlinear experience. The experience will vary with different people and groups. The definition, offered earlier, sets some parameters.

We would NOT be in dialogue if I focused on showing you how wrong you are, or tried to persuade you to accept my point of view without being willing to listen to your point of view, or if in a business, the boss told his subordinates that there was only one good way to sell their product, or in Congress, if one party refused to consider any solution to the immigration problem but theirs.

We are in a dialogue environment when we listen for what is meant and respond empathetically, ask questions to clarify and draw out the thinking of others, resist becoming defensive, acknowledge that on which we disagree but seek to find that on which we do agree, or when we are not trying to persuade but to discover, and when we find ourselves changing our views or positions in light of what we are discovering.

"Those who engage in dialogue," affirms Nancy Dixon, "must come to it with **humility, love, faith, and hope** – a formidable list of characteristics, but one that exemplifies a relational, rather than technique, perspective." (Dixon 1996)

A special kind of courage is required to engage in this *way to live*. It requires the courage to affirm our best nature, to actualize our potential, and to contribute to a society in which human energy can be put to constructive purposes. This kind of courage calls for a confidence empowered by a faith in an undergirding force that lifts, guides, and supports our initiatives for a relational, more than a transactional, way of life.

Something happens that can be healing, even transformational when we **empathetically relate to other people**. This healing happens between friends, lovers, therapists, and even between people with disagreements. We are rewarded when neurons in our brains connect to create empathy. Oxytocin, the hormone that creates warm feelings from close connections, can be released just when making eye contact. When empathy opens the gate, dialogue can emerge through questioning, listening, and reflection. Empathy enhances both perspective and relationships.

Neurons in our brains appear to cause us to mirror what we observe in others – how and why we can read people's thinking as well as feel empathy for them. These neurons are a key to how human beings survive and thrive in a complex social world.

Serious attention is required to practice this *way to live*. When our attention is focused on a dialogical exchange, we get a neural harmony - an interconnection among diverse brain areas. Paying serious attention puts our brains in the zone. Creating space where focused attention can thrive energizes a more open, responsive environment in which to explore.

Active listening is a way to help us move from simply hearing words to creating an exchange of meaning. It is difficult to listen. We lose interest. Our minds wander. We find ourselves "reacting" to what we hear or to the way that we hear it, rather than being open to meaning. Active listening is an absolute necessity for transformational dialogue. Questions can only be asked and dialogical responses given when serious listening is at work.

Questions that optimize dialogue do not put others on the defensive. Consider the difference between asking, "Why don't you agree with me?" and asking, "Is there something in my position with which you don't agree?" Or instead of saying, "You can't possibly mean that," say, "Can you understand how I might disagree with that?"

Dialogical questions evoke deeper perspective when we offer brief reflective comments to show that we understand. For example, we might confirm understanding by summarizing what has been said, and when appropriate, ask questions to seek clarification or encourage further exploration.

You will find many references to "active listening" if you Google it.

Nonverbal expressions can either reinforce the context for this kind of dialogical exchange or create the opposite effect. Eye contacts, smiles, frowns, nods, restlessness, leanings, and other wordless expressions of our interest and responses greatly impact the communication climate.

In his newsletter, Dan Schawbel shared an interview with professor and author Brené Brown whose TED talk, "**The Power of Vulnerability**," is one of the top five most-viewed TED talks in the world. Schawbel asked Brown why we have a crisis of disconnection in our society.

"The root cause of this disconnection," said Brown, "is our loss of a sense of true belonging that leads us to retreat to our bunkers. To change this, we must allow ourselves to be vulnerable, uncomfortable, and intentionally to be with people who are different from us."

Said Brown, "We're going to have to learn how to listen, have hard conversations, look for joy, share pain, and be more curious than defensive, all while seeking moments of togetherness.

"We have to create cultures where people feel safe — where their belonging is not threatened by speaking out, and they are supported when they make the decision to brave the wilderness, stand alone, and speak truth to bullshit while maintaining civility." (Brown 2017)

GUIDELINES FOR GROUP DIALOGUE

- A group of nine is optimal for dialogue; however, I have also had good experience with a few more and a few less.

- Omit a hierarchy of roles and references to external authorities.

- Discipline is needed to assure opportunity for all members to contribute. Invite those who hold back to speak out.

- Listen for what is *meant* instead of listening for what is correct or seeking agreement. What does the person who is speaking *mean*? What is that person's emerging "truth"?

- Assume that each member of the group has a piece of the answer to issues and that together the group can craft a new and better response.

- Disagreements should be shared. Validate disagreements as a different way of looking at a subject, rather than trying to strong-arm agreement.

- Celebrate new insights, deeper understandings, greater clarity as they occur.

David Bohm, Donald Factor, and Peter Garrett affirm in their *Notes on Dialogue*, "The spirit of dialogue is one of free play, a sort of collective dance of the mind that, nevertheless, has immense power and reveals coherent purpose. Once begun it becomes a continuing adventure that can open the way to significant and creative change." (Bohm, Factor, and Garrett 1991)

William Isaacs put it this way: "Rather than seeing our conversations as the crashing and careening of billiard balls, individuals may come to see and feel them as fields in which a sense of wholeness can appear, intensify, and diminish in intensity again." (Isaacs 1999)

BARRIERS TO THE PRACTICE OF DIALOGUE

- Different personalities sometimes rub against each other instead of seeking mutual discovery.

- Respect for one another can suppress openness.

- Some egos find dialog too confining.

- Rank and power can intimidate instead of liberate.

DIALOGUE LEADERSHIP INSTITUTE

ASSUMPTIONS:

- The practice of dialogue has widespread endorsement.

- The endorsement of dialogue has a long history.

- The practice of dialogue benefits people, organizations and society.

- Initiatives to encourage the practice of dialogue have short histories.

- There is little sustained support for the practice of dialogue.

Definition:
We are in a dialogue environment when we listen for what is meant and respond empathetically to what we hear, when we ask questions to clarify and draw out the thinking of others, when we resist being defensive, when

we acknowledge that on which we disagree but seek to find that on which we do agree, when we try to discover more than to persuade, when we find ourselves changing our views or positions in light of what we are discovering.

EXAMPLES OF CONTINUITY

From our beginnings as human beings, there has been a spiritual force that motivated people, communities, leaders and institutions. It is beyond us, yet it guides and empowers us to live with principles that sustain and enrich our lives. Religion has a bumpy history; however, continuity has persisted based on the needs met and the benefits discovered in the practice of a faith in a transcendent reality.

Alcoholics Anonymous is arguably the most successful recovery program in the world. Bill Wilson and Bob Smith founded it in 1935. Its members are anonymous. It does not have a bureaucratic, hierarchical structure.

Members are understood, listened to, encouraged, challenged, supported, and loved. AA is nonprofessional, self-supporting, multiracial, apolitical, and available almost everywhere.

"Membership is open to anyone who wants to do something about his or her drinking problem."

The total quality movement (TQM) sparked the economic revolution in Japan following WWII and spread across the world. Where seriously applied, TQM's applications generated better products, services, and profit. Competition and leadership contributed to TQM's progress. In addition, the applications that succeeded and endured were built on the dialogical engagement of all who needed to be involved.

The Dialogue Leadership Institute can be another example of an enterprise that is sustained because it meets a need like religion, alcoholism, and quality.

- The Institute needs to reach, enroll, and support leaders who will practice and advocate for dialogue.

- The Institute needs the long-term support of a foundation that extends beyond the support of an individual and short-term annual budgets.

HOW MIGHT A FOUNDATION APPROACH THIS MISSION?

1. Create and sustain the Dialogue Leadership Institute with an appropriate budget.

2. Provide a quarterly think-tank for invited leaders at which they will learn of the work of the Institute's initiatives, be invited to support those initiatives, and encouraged to join the Institute's Dialogue Leadership Network.

3. Provide an umbrella for organizations promoting dialogue. Sponsor a forum for these groups to dialogue about what they have in common and how they might use their combined resources to advance this mission.

4. Initiate articles on dialogue, including examples of its successful applications, for media publications.

5. Develop dialogue resources available to schools and colleges for courses and workshops.

6. Identify, equip, and facilitate the availability of effective advocates of dialogue for TV, radio, and social media.

7. Generate research on the practice of dialogue including big data research.

8. Seek international opportunities to promote dialogue.

9. Employ interns for the Institute:

   a. Two-year term (to maintain fresh and high energy leadership)

   b. Job responsibilities to include: direct, promote, and facilitate Institute programs

   c. Alternate between recent MBA graduates and recent Special Forces retirees

WHAT FOLLOWS IS THE PRODUCT OF OUR IMAGINATION.

What if a very good year for the Institute could include all of this?

Volume IX of *The Shirley River Quarterly* features dialogue. The volume title is "A Rising Tide." <u>These are the lead descriptions of the articles.</u>

- "Dialogue for All of Us," published by the Dialogue Leadership Institute, has in circulation 10,000 copies in English, 5,000 copies in Spanish, and 3,000 copies in Arabic.

- The *Algernon Monthly's* article on a course being offered in ten nursing schools on nursing dialogue led by former patients.

- Indian billionaire, Azim Shindai, endowed the Eastern Political Business School with scholarships for politicians to gain masters' degrees in political dialogue.

- A syndicate of dialogue training organizations now offers a State Department course on dialogical diplomacy.

- Twelve federal judges, trained by the Dialogue Leadership Institute, are volunteers in the Congressional Dialogue Facilitator Fellowship to facilitate dialogue for bipartisan legislators.

- Immigration legislation, stimulated by a bipartisan group facilitated by a Congressional Dialogue Facilitator Fellowship judge, was passed.

- Twelve high schools offer courses on transformational dialogue.

- Facilitated by interns of the Dialogue Leadership Institute, seven students and a professor from the River's Edge Palestinian College and seven students and a professor from the Next Steps College in Israel are working on a grass roots peace plan for their nations.

- Professor Kim Vandenburg of Green College conducted a big data analysis on the curriculum seeds of dialogue practiced in American private colleges.

- Privately held Marketing Encounters offers its clients a unique strategy for employing dialogue in its marketing.

- The Dialogue Leadership Institute's Leadership Think-Tank offers dialogue training by its leaders for corporate executives.

- A task force from three state universities is evaluating the progress of the Dialogue Leadership Institute's initiatives.

The *Shirley River Quarterly* reports that a record number of their "Rising Tide" issue has been purchased including seven schools, five corporations, three national newspapers and three television networks. Three additional printings have been required to meet this demand.

ACKNOWLEDGEMENTS

The many named in the previous chapters contributed to my knowledge of and experience with transformational dialogue. I am especially indebted to those with whom I shared an experience of transformational dialogue. It has been a life and career of exploration and discovery with kindred spirits. We have stretched together. We have served together. We have been rewarded together.

Farheen Naveed included her many international connections in our survey that made it global in scope.

Jacqueline Stevens brought her professional skills and gracious empathy to edit and re-edit my attempts to express what I wish to convey in my dialogue mission.

My fellow Directors of The Living Dialog Ministries give me an abundance of support for this mission, for which I am deeply grateful.

Dear friends wrote checks to underwrite expenses required to take many of the steps in this journey.

Many beloved members of my family give me encouragement as well as material and personal support.

Director of Pastoral Care, Rev. Dr. Lynn McClintock, at Westminster-Canterbury Richmond, and her colleagues graciously hosted my lecture on "The Awesome Benefits of Transformational Dialogue." Farheen Naveed led the post-lecture dialogue. Members of my family and a colleague produced the video now on YouTube (Irving Stubbs dialogue).

My mission to encourage the practice of transformational dialogue is a spiritual mission. I believe that God made us to explore, to discover, to stretch, to serve and in all of that to be made whole. The journey has not always been smooth, but I have always felt the lift of sustaining arms and the encouragement of a guiding presence.

CPSIA information can be obtained
at www.ICGtesting.com
Printed in the USA
BVHW050909080623
665611BV00003B/107